Origami Boxes

Tomoko Fuse

CHIKUMA SHOBO/JAPAN PUBLICATIONS

Tokyo, Japan

Left, *tsuzura* 〔lid : pp. 12 − 15 ; base : pp. 16 − 18〕
Right, variation, a smaller *tsuzura*. Basically units are folded
almost in the same way as the larger one, except that you
begin with a diagonal instead of a line that divides side lines in
half.

Square boxes : below, 'bow knot'; right, 'wheel'; above,
'lightning' (lids : pp. 24 – 26 ; base : pp. 19 – 23).

Lids of square boxes : with 'pinwheels' on both sides
(pp. 34 – 40).
The base below right has the same pattern as *B* on
p. 33.

Above, lid of a square box :
'lozenge' (pp. 27 – 28).
Below, bases of a square
box : left to right, A ; C ;
combination of A and C
(pp. 30 – 33).

Center, lid of a square box : 'fancy pinwheel' (pp. 41-43). The other four lids are variations and are folded differently from ⑩ on p. 36.

Above left, lid of an octagon box : 'little
flower' (pp.44-46) made of *chiyogami*
(colorful paper). Right, base (pp. 50-54).
The box contains four folded inserts that
fit nicely.
Below, lid of an octagon box : 'double
stars' (pp. 47-49).

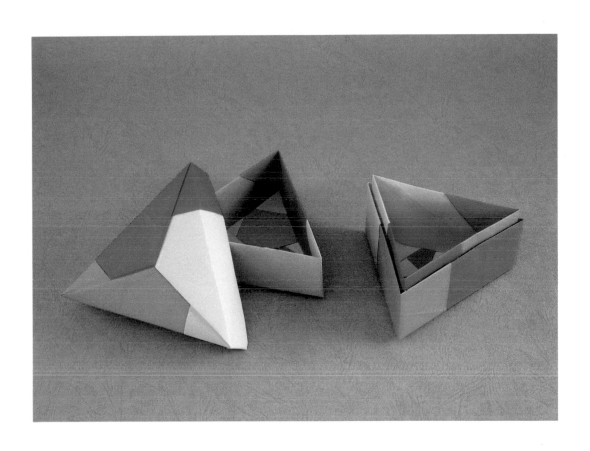

Triangle boxes (pp. 55–61).

Above left, lid of a hexagon box : 'six-petal pinwheel' (pp. 62-65 ; base : pp. 68-71). By devising different ways of folding, you can make a seven- or eight-sided box.
Below, lid of a hexagon box : 'flower and star' (pp. 66-67).

Contents

Preface

Unit origami is a new way of folding paper, then joining the parts
to form objects — in this case, boxes — still without using
scissors or paste, of course!

Folding these units is relatively simple, and joining the parts
together is like solving a riddle.

While you can make many fanciful objects with unit origami,
this book is a collection of the beautiful boxes you can make.
You'll discover the lovely, intricate patterns than can only be made
with origami. And you may find, as I have, that units joined
differently make different patterns.

So experiment, and make wonderful boxes of your own by using
different colors, different papers, and thinking as you work of the
special things you'll want to keep in these boxes.

Signs used in the illustrations

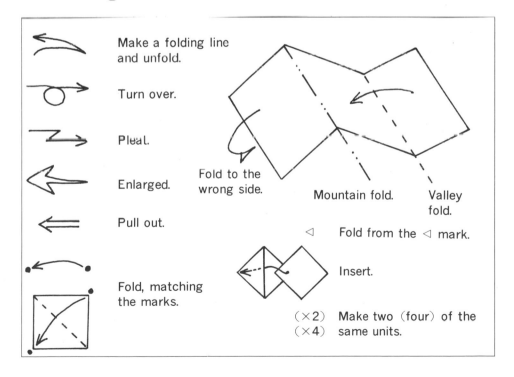

Make a folding line and unfold.

Turn over.

Pleat.

Enlarged.

Pull out.

Fold, matching the marks.

Fold to the wrong side.

Mountain fold.

Valley fold.

◁   Fold from the ◁ mark.

Insert.

(×2) Make two (four) of the
(×4) same units.

Lid of *tsuzura* (wicker clothes-box)

By folding according to *A*, you can produce this pattern on the lid. *B* is plain. Both are made of two pieces of paper.

(For the base of the box that matches these lids, see pp. 16–18.)

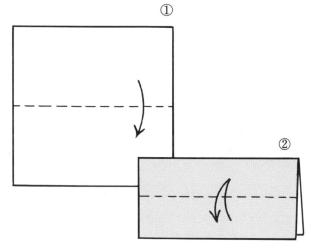

① ②

Mark a folding line on the upper layer only.

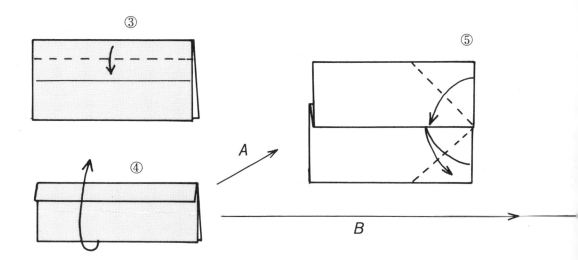

③

④

⑤

A

B

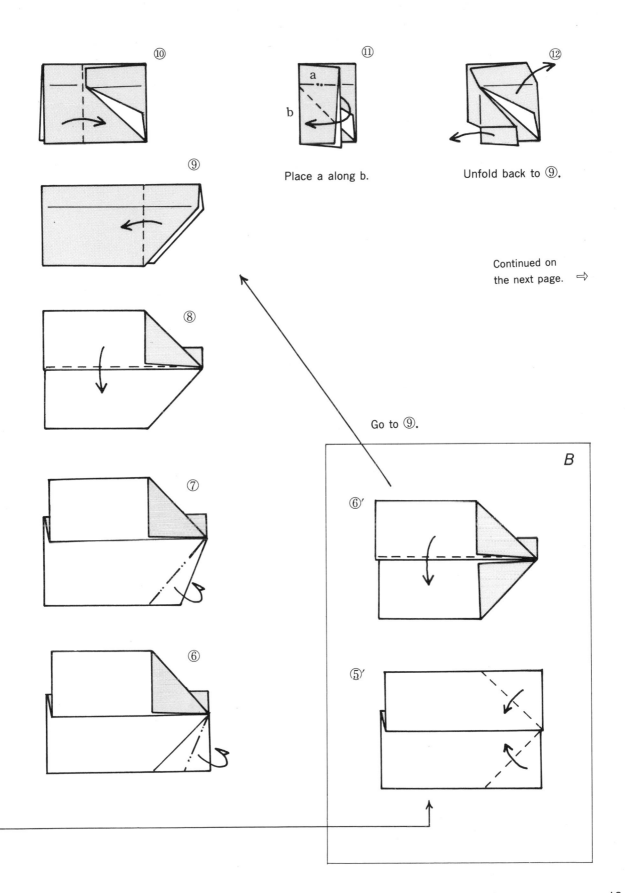

⑩

⑪ Place a along b.

a

b

⑫ Unfold back to ⑨.

⑨

Continued on the next page. ⇨

⑧

Go to ⑨.

B

⑦

⑥'

⑥

⑤'

13

⑬

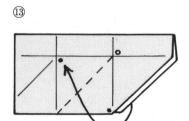

Fold up to the ○ mark,
matching ● marks.

⑭

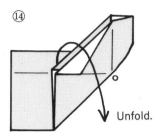

Unfold.

⑮

Fold the upper
layer only.

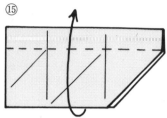

⑰

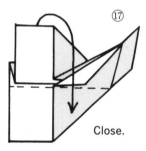

Close.

⑯

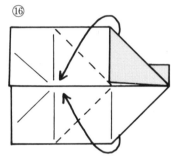

Make the right
side stand upright.

90°
▽

⑱

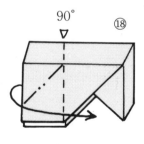

Pleat along
the lines
already marked.

⑲

Fold along
the center line.

Finished unit.

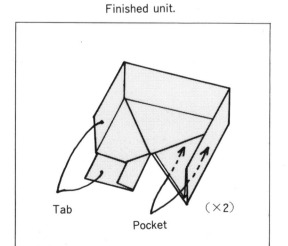

Tab

Pocket

(×2)

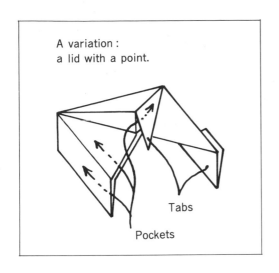

A variation :
a lid with a point.

Tabs

Pockets

By changing the folding a little as illustrated, you can make a lid with a raised point like the above photo. See if you can make it.

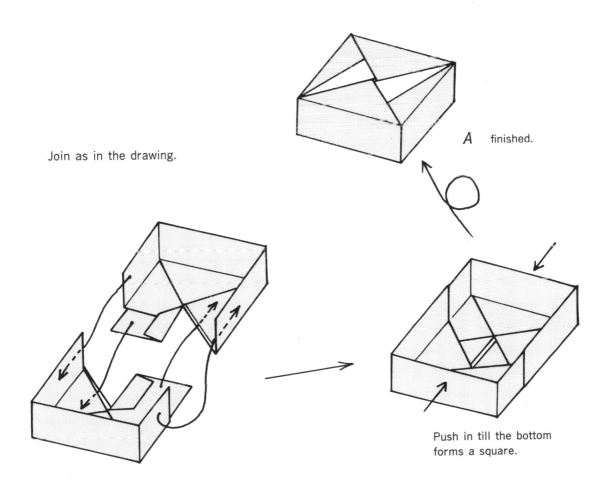

Join as in the drawing.

A finished.

Push in till the bottom forms a square.

Base of *tsuzura*

I am very fond of this crisp little
box. Its folds look so simple, but
try separating the units for a
friend and ask them to reassemble
the base of the box. It's quite a
brain teaser !

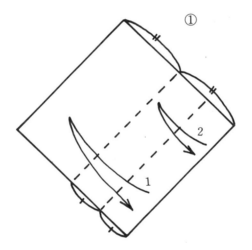

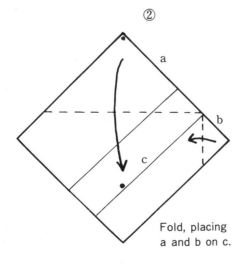

Fold, placing
a and b on c.

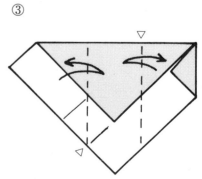

Fold at ◁ marks and unfold.

⑨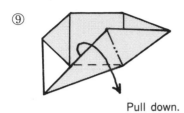

Pull down.

⑩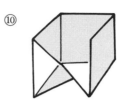

⑧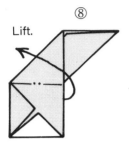

Lift.

To join the units,
see the next page.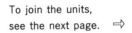

⑦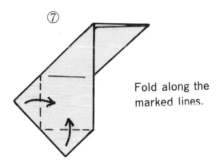

Fold along the
marked lines.

⑥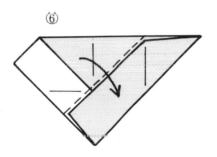

④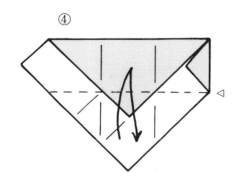

⑤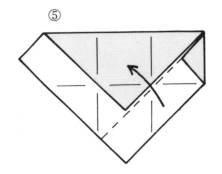

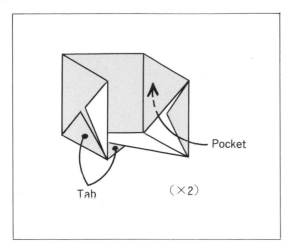

Pocket

Tab   (×2)

Finished unit.

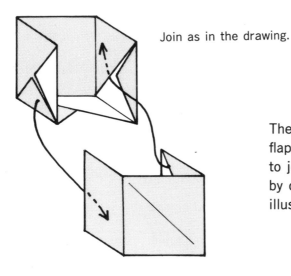

Join as in the drawing.

The units with their loose flaps may be a little difficult to join. See if you can do it by carefully following the illustrations.

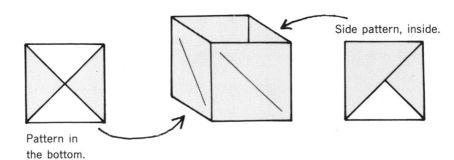

Side pattern, inside.

Pattern in the bottom.

Square boxes : first series

Left to right: 'lightning' (p. 23), 'bow knot' (p. 22), 'wheel' (p. 21).

By just joining the same units differently you will find that new patterns appear like magic. Here are two such patterns, and a third, a combination of the first two.

Both folding and joining are very simple. We use four units. Let us first fold the units as follows.

①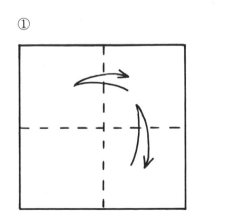

②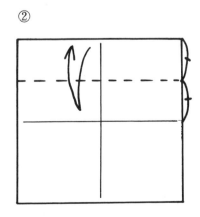

⇨ Continued on the next page.

③

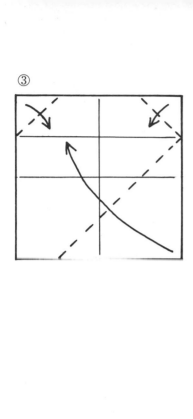

④

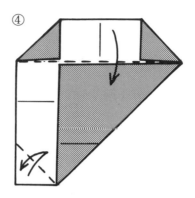

⑤

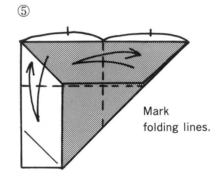

Mark
folding lines.

⑥

Fold up to the ○ mark.

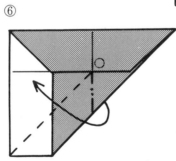

Join as in the drawing. ⤸

⑦

90°

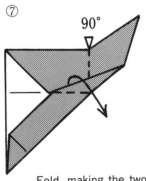

Fold, making the two
sides stand upright.

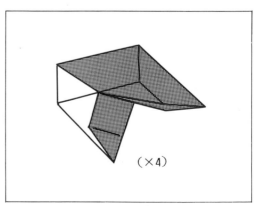

(×4)

Finished unit.

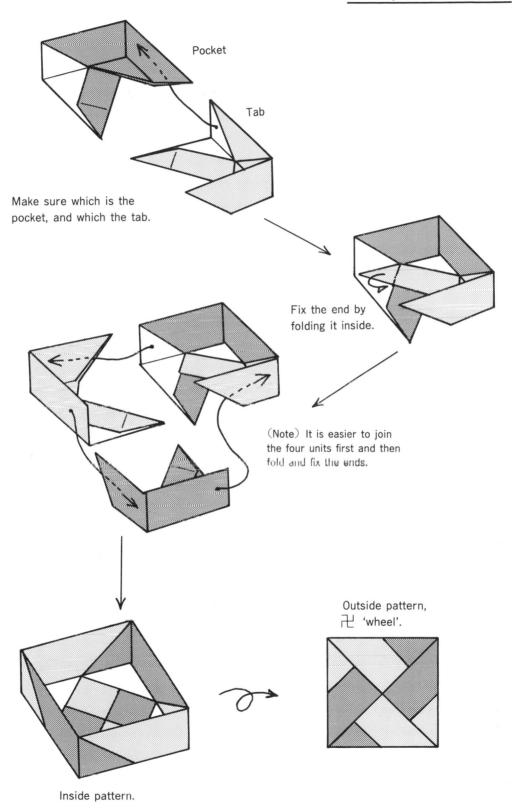

Pocket

Tab

Make sure which is the
pocket, and which the tab.

Fix the end by
folding it inside.

（Note）It is easier to join
the four units first and then
fold and fix the ends.

Inside pattern.

Outside pattern,
卍 'wheel'.

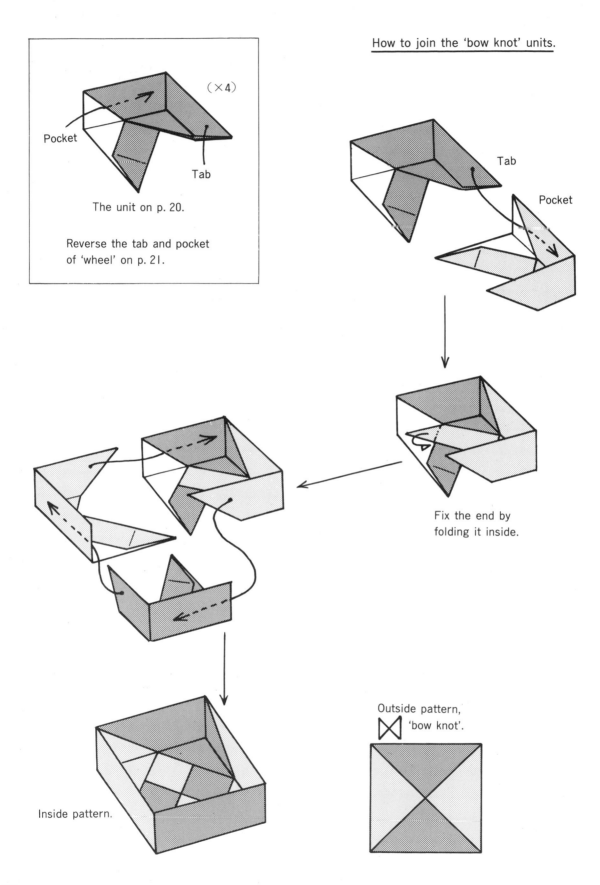

(×4)

Pocket

Tab

The unit on p. 20.

Reverse the tab and pocket
of 'wheel' on p. 21.

Tab

Pocket

Fix the end by
folding it inside.

Inside pattern.

Outside pattern,
'bow knot'.

How to join the 'lightning' units.

Unlike the 'wheel' and 'bow knot', the units that make the 'lightning' pattern
are joined by using both ends of two units as tabs, and both ends of
remaining two units as pockets.

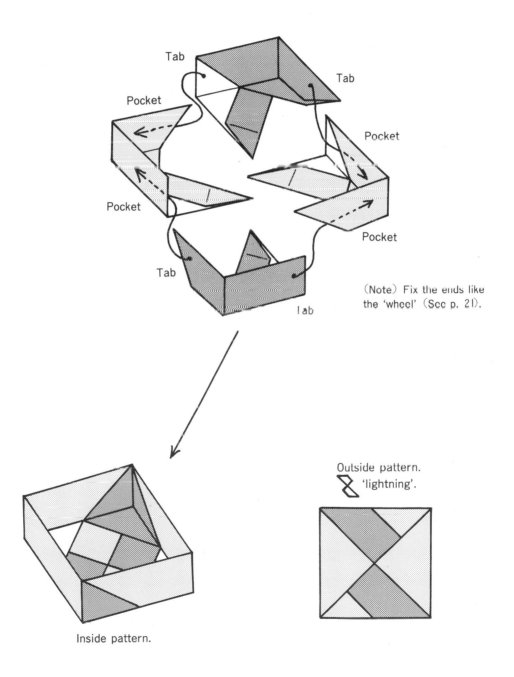

Tab

Tab

Pocket

Pocket

Pocket

Pocket

Tab

Tab

(Note) Fix the ends like
the 'wheel' (See p. 21).

Outside pattern.
'lightning'.

Inside pattern.

Lids of square boxes

© 1986

Now let us make lids for the boxes we have made. As with the boxes, two different lid patterns can be made from the same units, and their combination makes a third pattern. The outside patterns of the lids match those of the boxes.

The joining of the third pattern is not illustrated, but it is the same as the joining of the lightning-patterned box on p. 23.

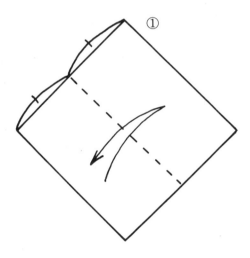

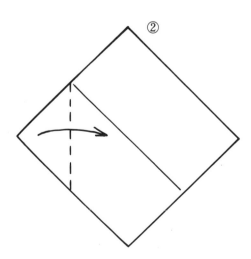

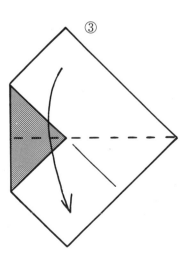

Finished units.

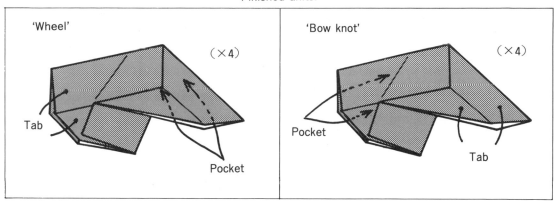

'Wheel' (×4)

Tab

Pocket

'Bow knot' (×4)

Pocket

Tab

⑧

90°

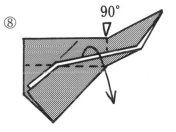

Fold, making the sides
stand upright as above.

For joining,
see the next page. ⇨

⑦

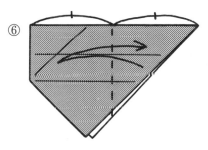

Fold up to the
○ mark.

⑥

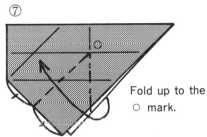

Mark a folding
line on the
upper layer only.

④

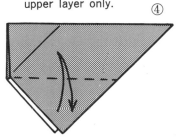

⑤

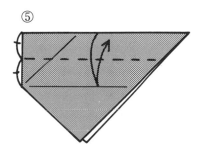

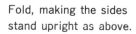

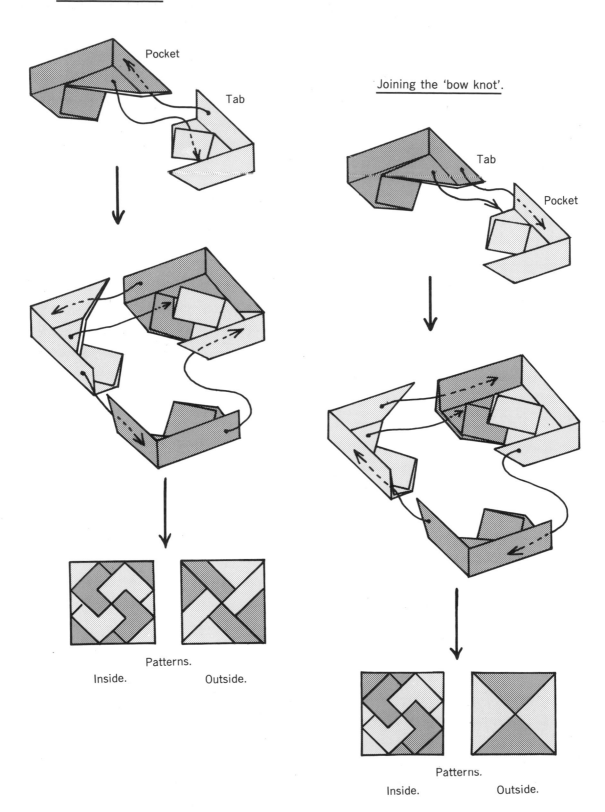

Joining the 'wheel'.

Pocket

Tab

Joining the 'bow knot'.

Tab

Pocket

Patterns.

Inside.

Outside.

Patterns.

Inside.

Outside.

Lid of a square box. Variation : lozenge

© 1986

At a certain point (④), change the folding on page 25 slightly and you will have a lid with a different pattern.

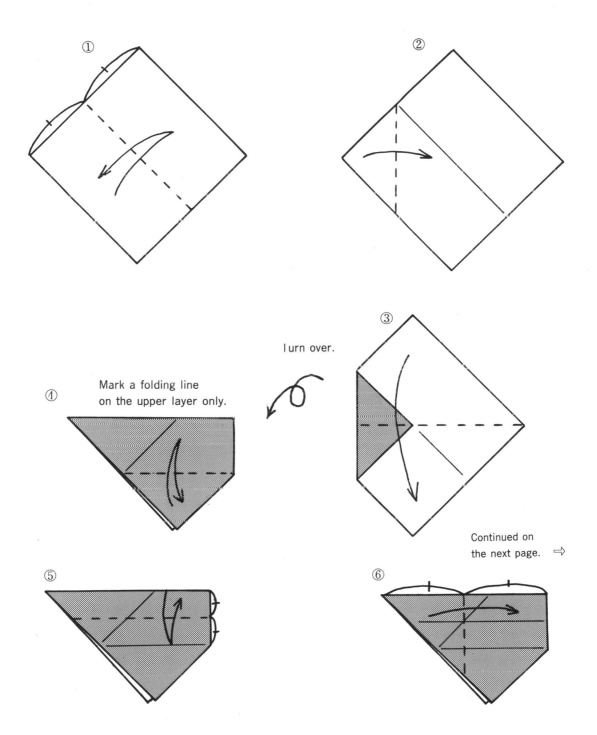

①

②

Turn over.

③

④ Mark a folding line on the upper layer only.

⑤

⑥

Continued on the next page. ⇨

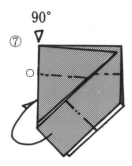

90°

⑦

○

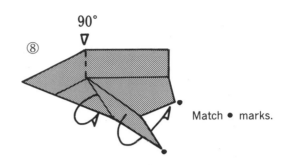

90°

⑧

Match ● marks.

Fold the marked line to the wrong side, up to the ○ mark, matching ● marks in ⑧. Fold only the inner layers.

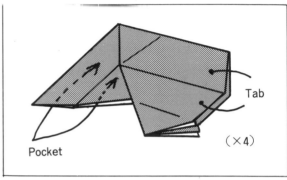

Tab

Pocket

(×4)

Finished unit.

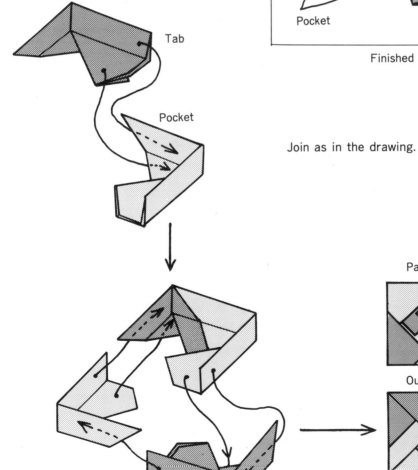

Tab

Pocket

Join as in the drawing.

Patterns.

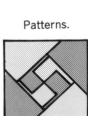

Outside.

Inside.

'Bow knot' (p. 26).

'Lightning'.

'Wheel' (p. 26).

'Lozenge' (p. 28).

Square boxes : second series

© 1988

Fold as illustrated. You can make three different patterns, *A, B* and *C.* It is all very simple, and such fun !

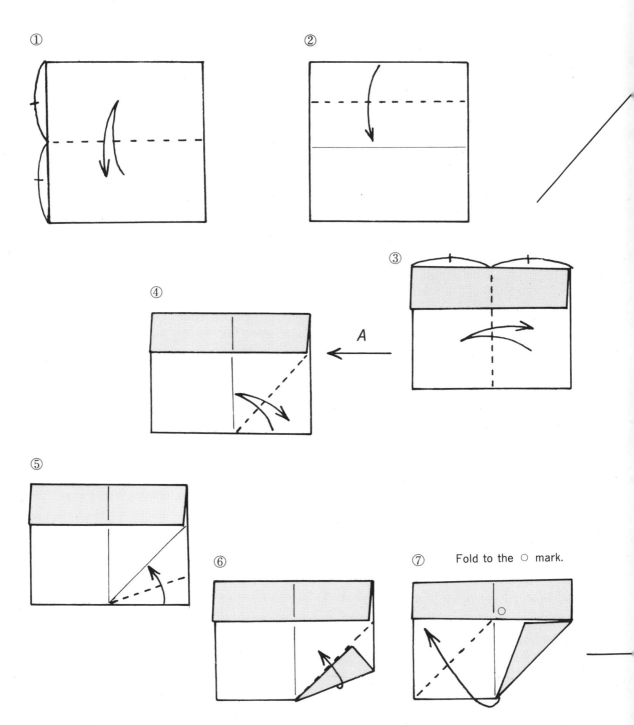

① ②

③

④

A

⑤

⑥

⑦ Fold to the ○ mark.

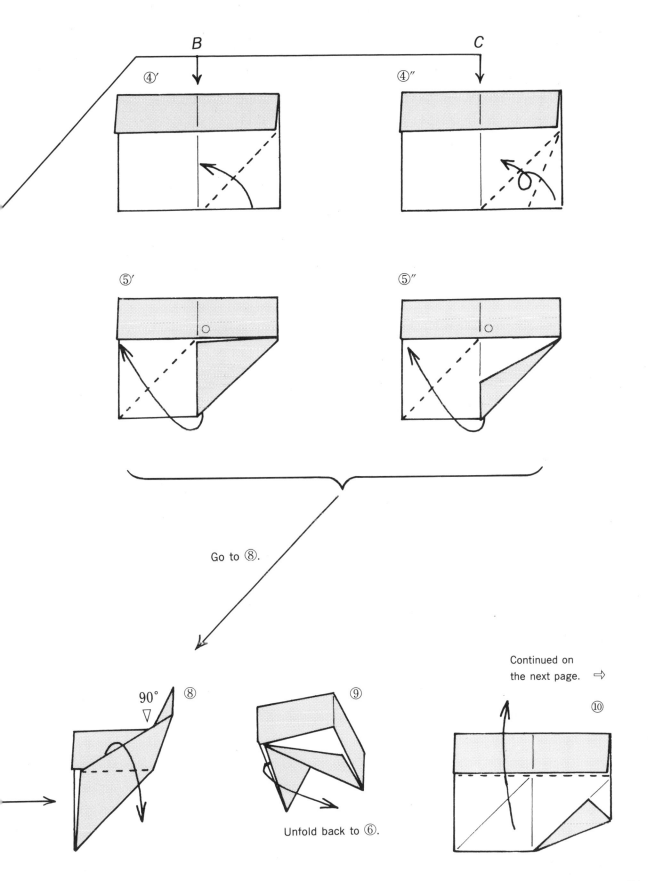

B

C

④′

④″

⑤′

⑤″

Go to ⑧.

Continued on
the next page. ⇨

90°
⑧

⑨

⑩

Untold back to ⑥.

⑪

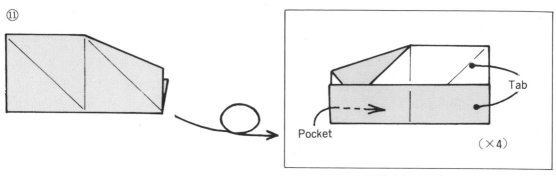

Finished unit.

(×4)

Tab

Pocket

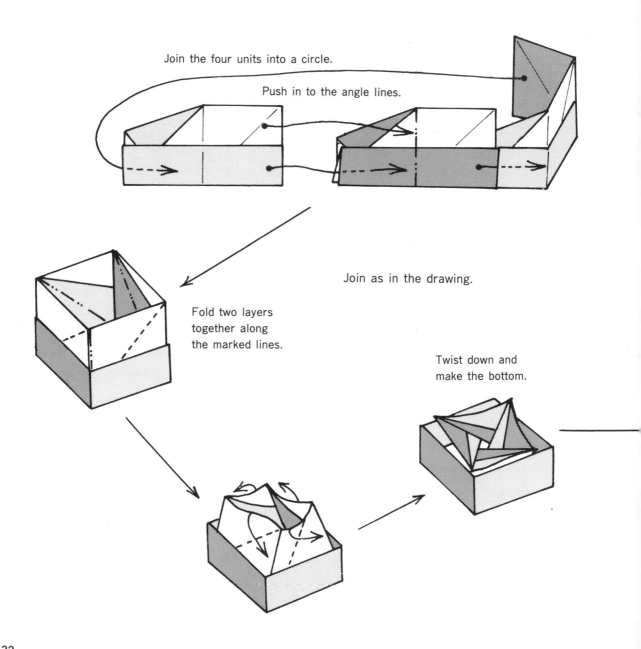

Join the four units into a circle.

Push in to the angle lines.

Join as in the drawing.

Fold two layers
together along
the marked lines.

Twist down and
make the bottom.

A

B

Ĉ

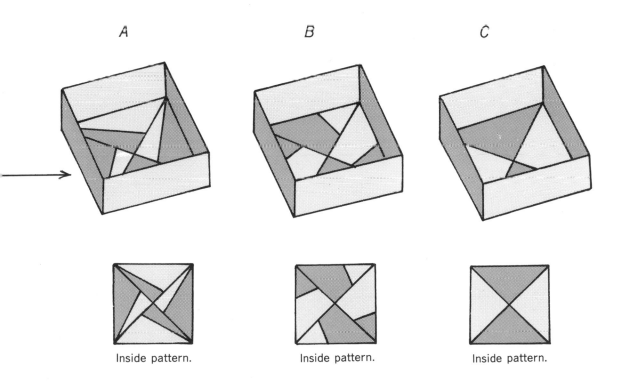

Inside pattern.

Inside pattern.

Inside pattern.

33

Lids of square boxes with pinwheels on both sides

Left to right : combination of *A* and *B*, *B*, *A*.

These lids have pinwheel patterns inside and outside. The joined *A*- and *B*- types are illustrated here, but you can join the units so that you have different patterns inside and out. You can also finish the main pattern in different ways. Experiment!

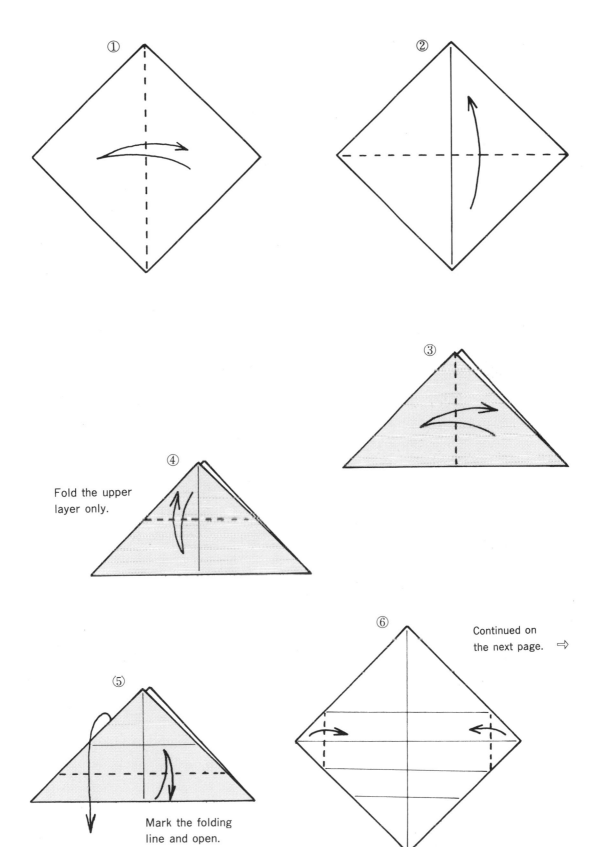

① ②

③

④ Fold the upper layer only.

⑤ Mark the folding line and open.

⑥

Continued on the next page. ⇨

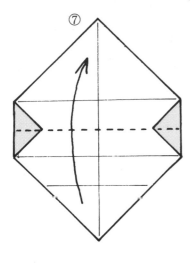

⑦

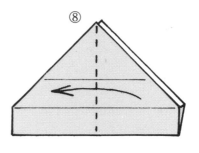

⑧

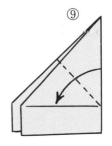

⑨

Reverse
the position.

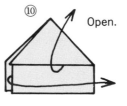

⑩ Open.

⑪

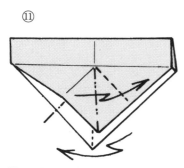

Pleat the upper and lower layers.

⑫

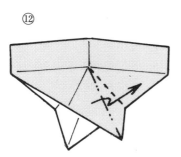

Making the pleat.

⑬

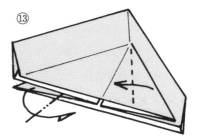

Ordinary boxes have no designs on the bottom or inside their lids, but with unit origami you can make boxes with these wonderful patterns on inner surfaces. The pleasure on first seeing these charming little boxes increases when you look inside! This delight in finding unexpected patterns is the result of unit origami.

To join the units,
see the next page. ⇨

Finished unit.

⑭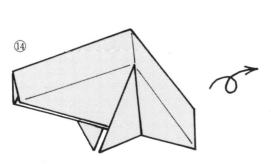

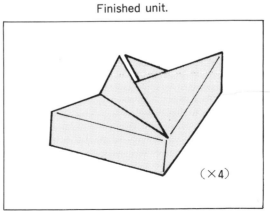

(×4)

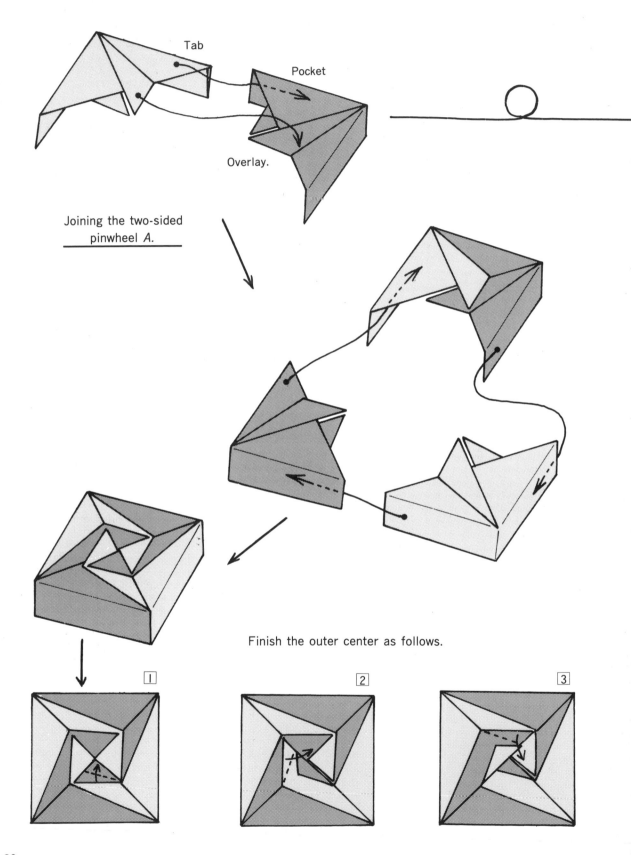

Tab

Pocket

Overlay.

Joining the two-sided pinwheel A.

Finish the outer center as follows.

1

2

3

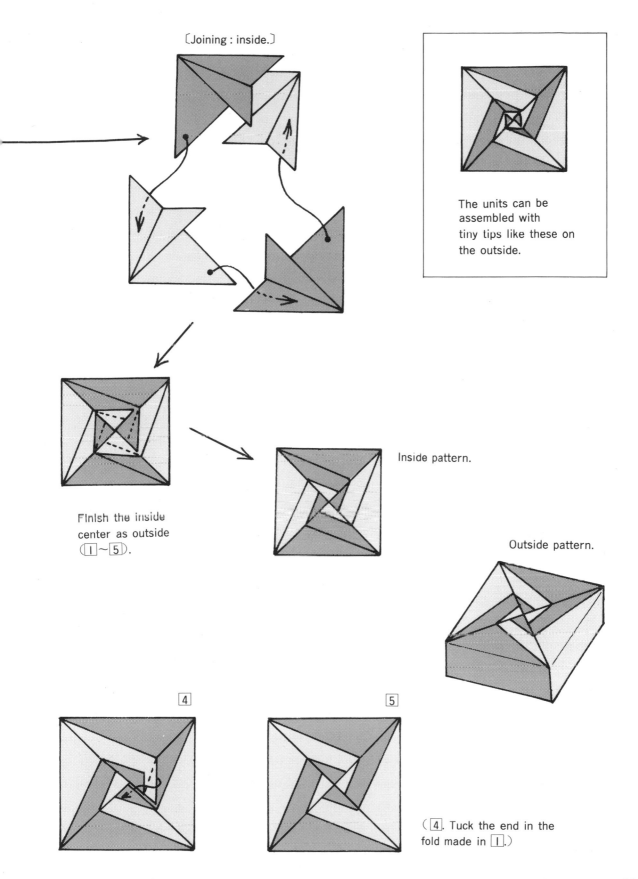

[Joining : inside.]

The units can be assembled with tiny tips like these on the outside.

Inside pattern.

Outside pattern.

Finish the inside center as outside ⬚1~⬚5.

⬚4

⬚5

(⬚4. Tuck the end in the fold made in ⬚1.)

39

Joining two-sided pinwheel *B*.

[Joining outside.]

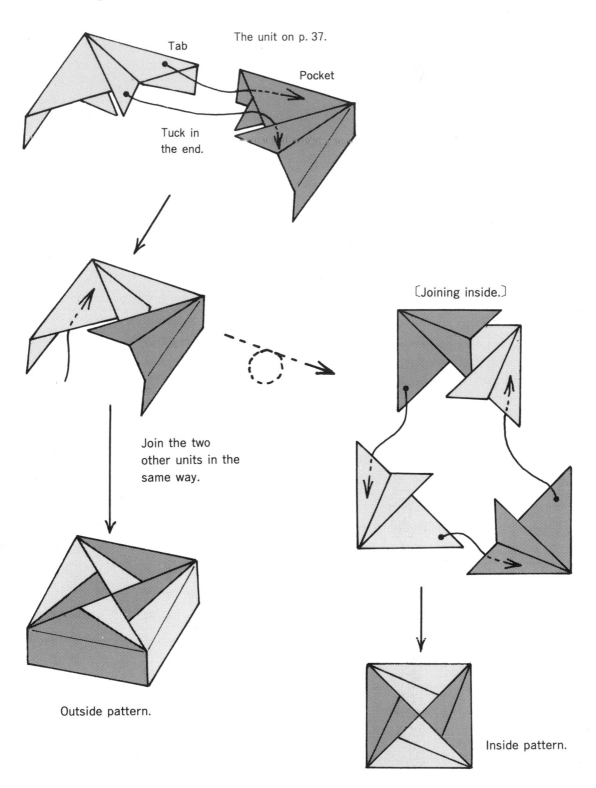

The unit on p. 37.

Tab

Pocket

Tuck in
the end.

Join the two
other units in the
same way.

[Joining inside.]

Outside pattern.

Inside pattern.

Lid of a square box : fancy pinwheel

© 1988

To make this lid, you fold and join in almost the same way as has already
been done (pp. 34-40), but the result is something unique. For best effect,
use paper with one side colored differently than the other.

From ⑩ on p. 36.

①

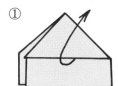

②

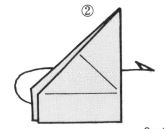

Continued on
the next page. ⇨

③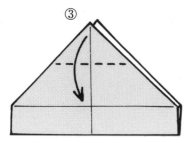

Fold the upper layer only.

④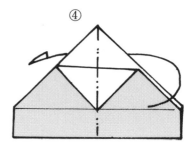

Fold along the center line.

⑤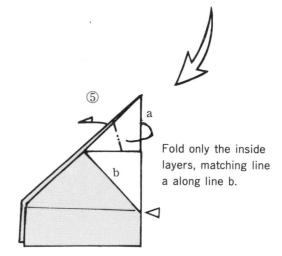

Fold only the inside layers, matching line a along line b.

⑥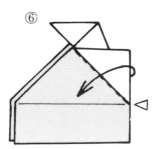

⑦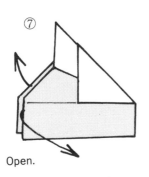

Open.

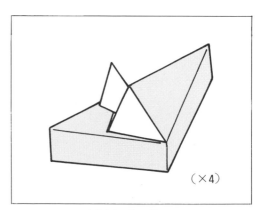

(×4)

Finished unit.

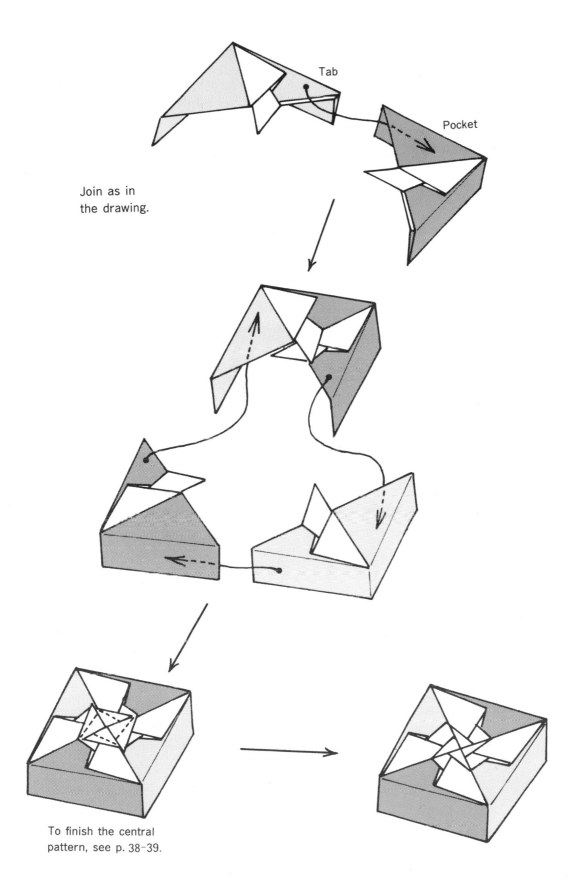

Tab

Pocket

Join as in
the drawing.

To finish the central
pattern, see p. 38-39.

Lid of an octagon box : little flower

(To fold the base, refer to p. 50.)

Now let us make an octagon lid, using four units. When the lid is joined, the white back of the paper appears in the center like a little flower, hence the box's name.

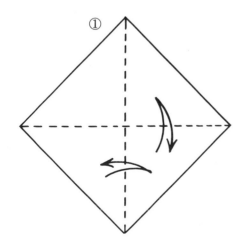

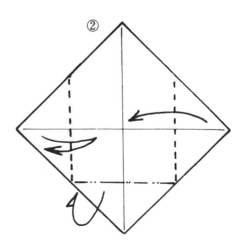

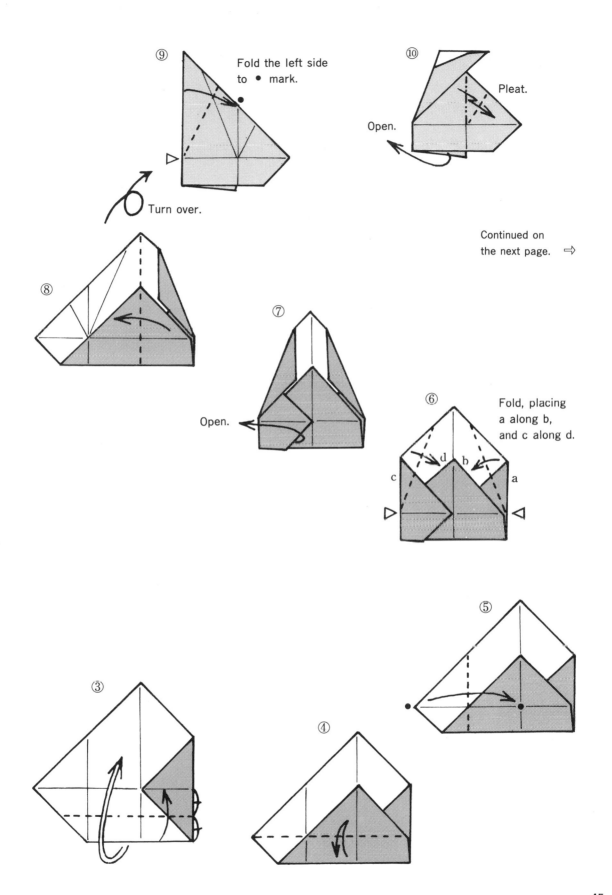

⑨ Fold the left side to ● mark.

Turn over.

⑩ Pleat.

Open.

Continued on the next page. ⇨

⑧

⑦ Open.

⑥ Fold, placing a along b, and c along d.

c   d   b   a

⑤

③

④

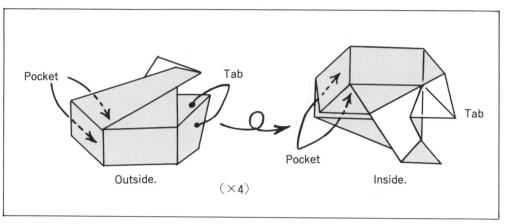

Pocket

Tab

Outside.

(×4)

Tab

Pocket

Inside.

Finished unit.

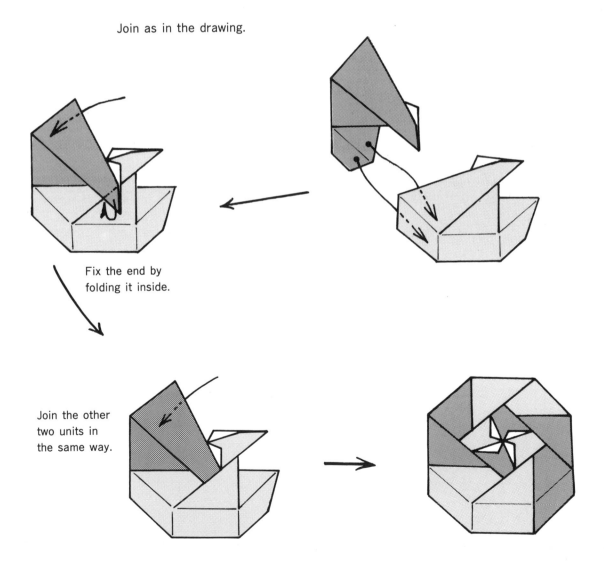

Join as in the drawing.

Fix the end by folding it inside.

Join the other two units in the same way.

Lid of an octagon box : double stars

© 1983

Fold the 'little flower' units inside out, and you will see the birth of twin stars, one colored, the other white. You can create such a change by just reversing the folding. Such is the fascination of origami! The little flower had the twin stars hidden in it.

①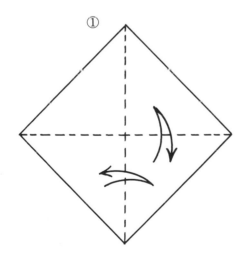

②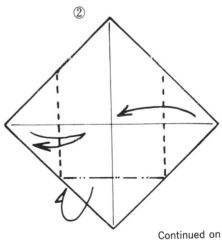

Continued on the next page. ⇨

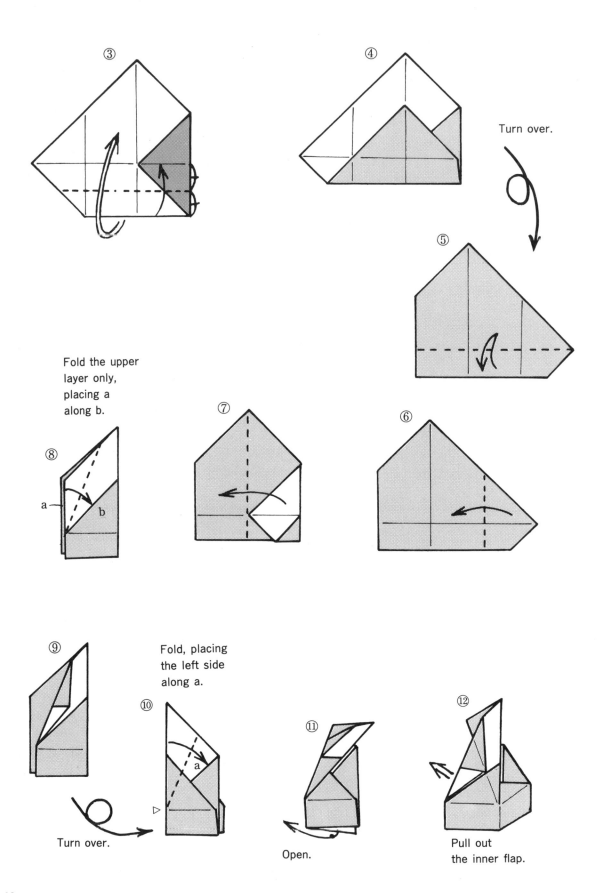

③

④

Turn over.

⑤

Fold the upper
layer only,
placing a
along b.

⑦

⑥

⑧

a

b

⑨

Fold, placing
the left side
along a.

⑩

a

▷

Turn over.

⑪

Open.

⑫

Pull out
the inner flap.

Join the other two units
in the same way.

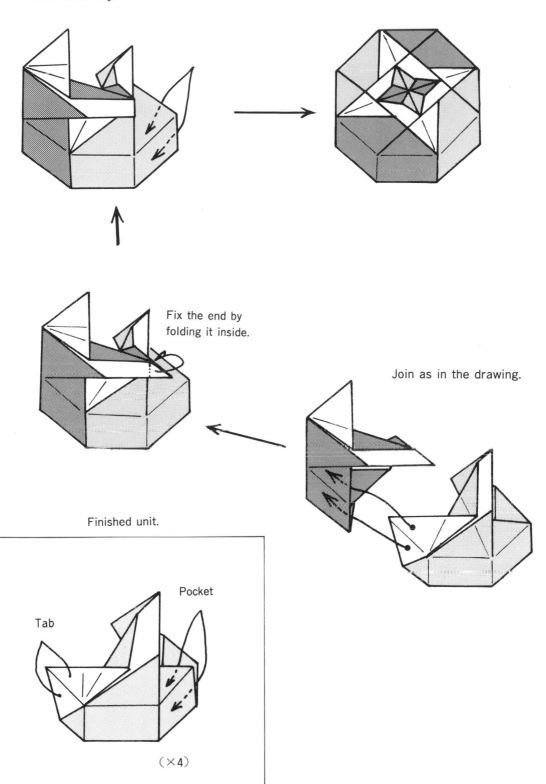

Fix the end by
folding it inside.

Join as in the drawing.

Finished unit.

Tab

Pocket

(×4)

Base of an octagon box

© 1988

The base of this box is rather complicated both to fold and to join. You fold and unfold at many places. Proceed slowly and with patience, carefully following the illustrations.

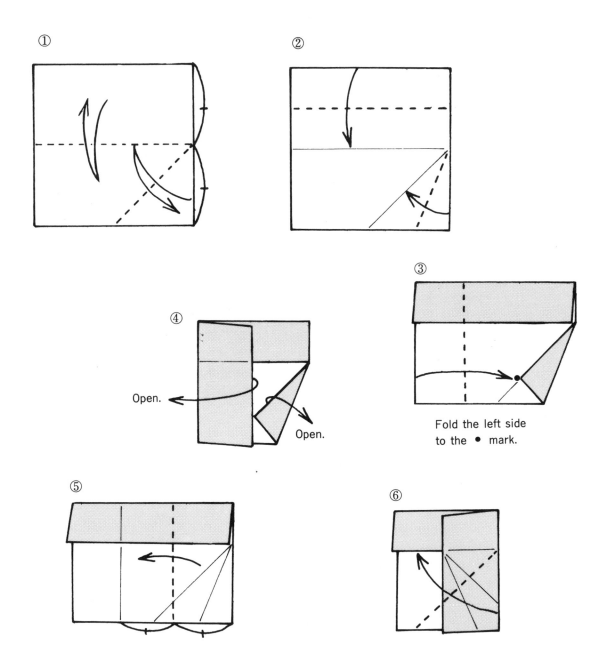

①

②

③ Fold the left side to the ● mark.

④ Open. Open.

⑤

⑥

⑫

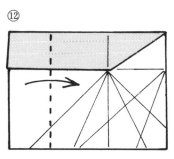

Fold along the line
marked in ③.

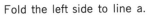
A narrow opening.

⑬

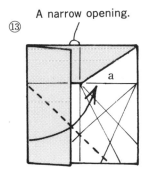
a

Fold the left side to line a.

⇨
Continued on
the next page.

⑪

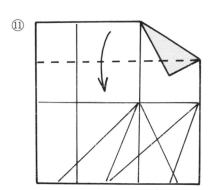

Fold along the line
marked in ②.

⑩

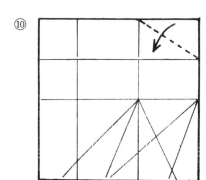

⑨

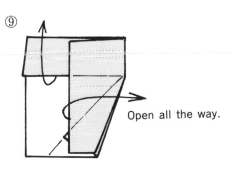

Open all the way.

⑧

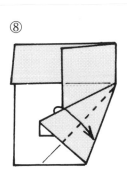

⑦

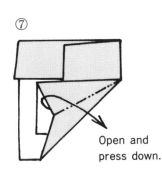

Open and
press down.

⑭

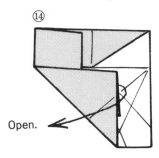

Open.

⑮

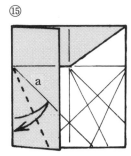

Fold the left side along
line a and then unfold.

⑯

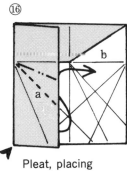

Pleat, placing
a along line b.

Fold along this line.

⑰

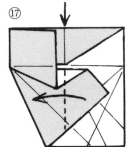

⑱

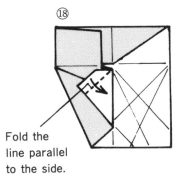

Fold the
line parallel
to the side.

⑲

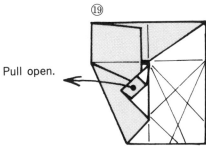

Pull open.

⑳

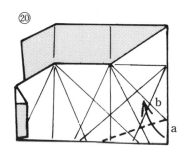

Place a along line b.

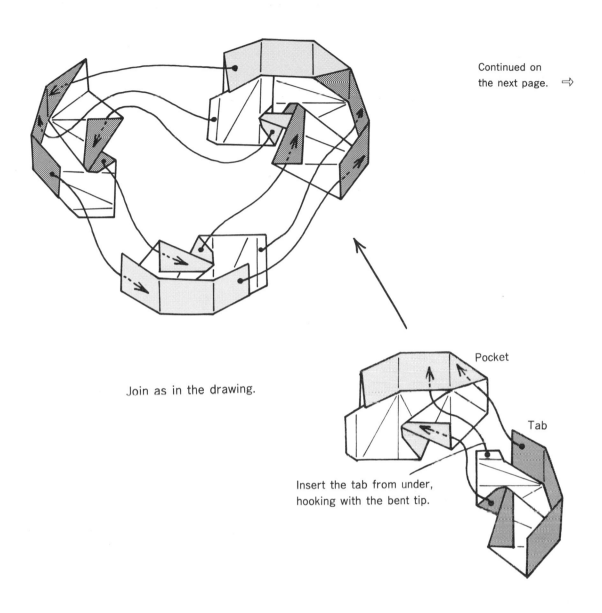

Continued on the next page. ⇨

Join as in the drawing.

Pocket

Tab

Insert the tab from under,
hooking with the bent tip.

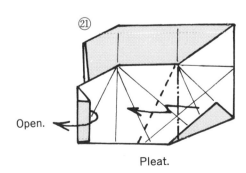

㉑

Open.

Pleat.

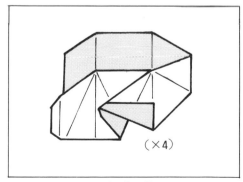

(×4)

Finished unit.

〔Finish : inside.〕

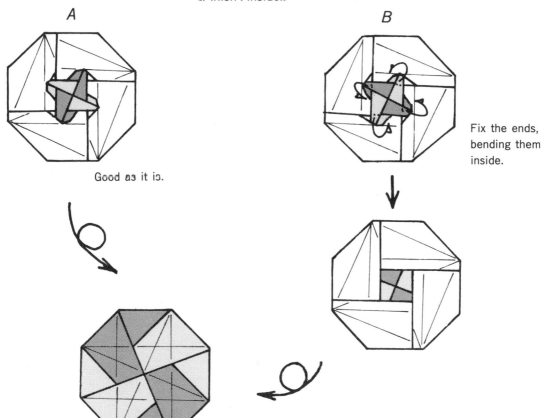

A

Good as it is.

B

Fix the ends,
bending them
inside.

Outside pattern.

Inside pattern of A.

54

Triangle box : medium size

© 1983

We seldom come across a triangle box, but with units of folded paper we can make wonderful ones. Let us make three such boxes of different sizes and use larger ones as lids.

Continued on the next page. ⇨

①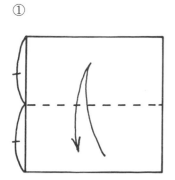

②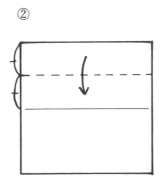

③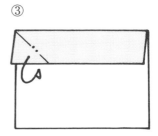

④

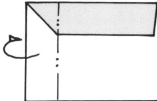

⑤

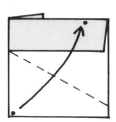

Match the bottom
left corner to the
top line.

⑥

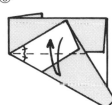

Mark the folding line
and unfold to ④.

⑦

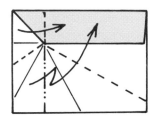

Fold correctly.

⑧

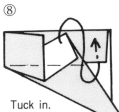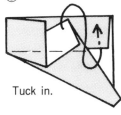

Tuck in.

⑨

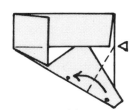

Fold, matching
the dotted lines.

⑩

Lift.

Open.

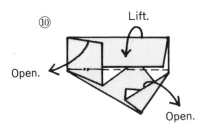

Open.

Unit of the medium box finished.

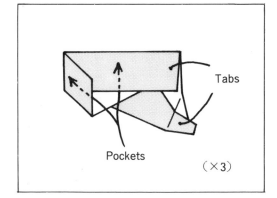

Tabs

Pockets

(×3)

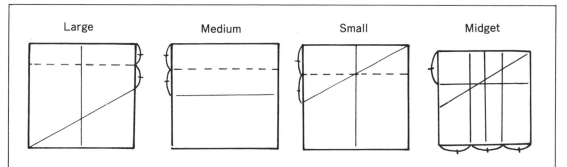

Large	Medium	Small	Midget

These illustrations show at a glance how triangle boxes of different sizes are folded. By changing folding lines you can change the depth of the box, and thus make boxes of four different sizes, large, medium, small and midget, all of which can be neatly placed one inside another. This is done without cutting the paper, and the folding involves no such ambiguity as sliding a folding line just a little. Triangle boxes made from square pieces of paper, boxes that can be contained one inside another, such are the wonders of origami !

Folding of 'Midget' is not shown here. The method is similar to the small box. You can make it without difficulty.

Join as in the drawing.

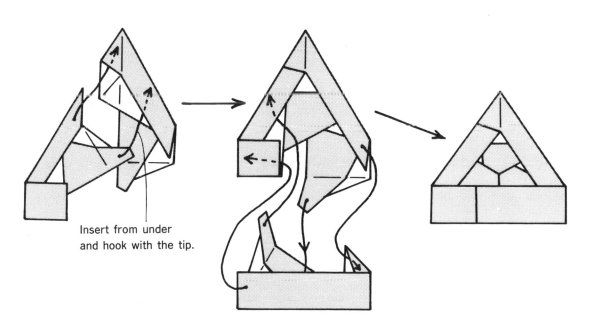

Insert from under and hook with the tip.

Triangle box : large size

© 1983

①

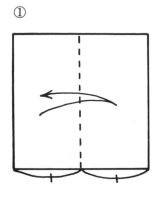

②

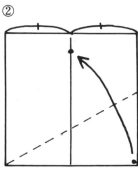

Match the bottom right
corner to the center line.

③

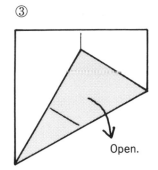

Open.

④

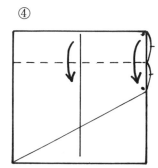

⑤

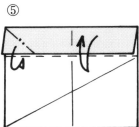

⑥

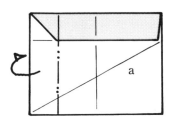

a

⑦

Fold along
line a in ⑥.

⑧

1

2

Open.

Unit of large-sized box finished.

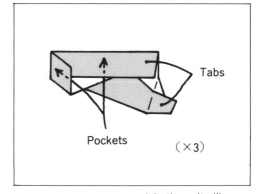

Tabs

Pockets

(×3)

Join the units like
the middle-sized box.
(See p. 57.)

⑮

Lift.

Open.

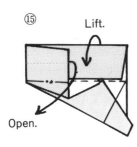

⑭

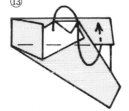

Fold, matching the divided
bottom lines, then unfold.

Fold 1 in ⑪ and
tuck inside.

⑬

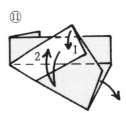

⑫

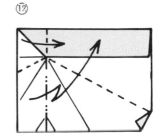

⑪

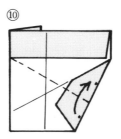

Mark the folding line,
then unfold to ⑥
with b folded as in ⑨.

⑨

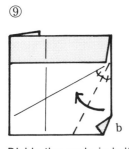

b

Divide the angle in half.

⑩

Fold, matching
the dotted lines.

Triangle box : small size

© 1983

①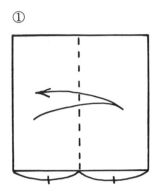

②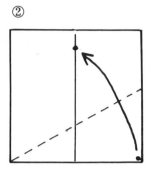

Match the bottom right corner to the center line.

③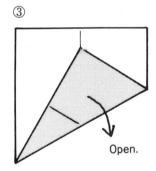

Open.

④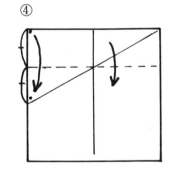

Turn upside down.

⑤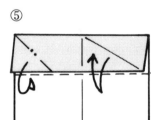

⑥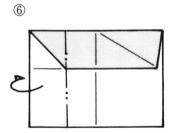

⑦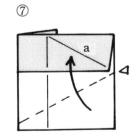

Fold the right side along the marked line a.

⑧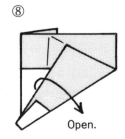

Open.

⑮

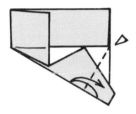

Open.

Unit of small box finished.

Tabs

Pockets

(×3)

Join the units like
the middle-sized box.
(See p. 57.)

⑭

Fold, matching the
divided bottom lines
and unfold.

⑬   Tuck inside.

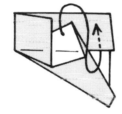

⑫

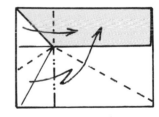

⑪

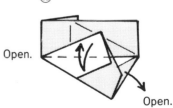

Open.

Open.

Mark the folding
line and unfold to ⑥.

⑨

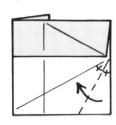

Divide the angle in half.

⑩

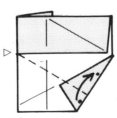

Fold, matching the
dotted lines.

61

Lid of a hexagon box with six-petal pinwheel © 1988

Now let us make a hexagon box. When the units are assembled, the white back of the paper appears in a clear-cut flower pattern.

①
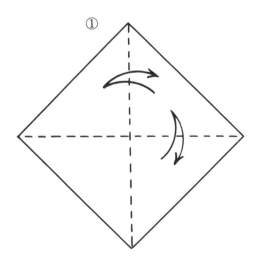

②
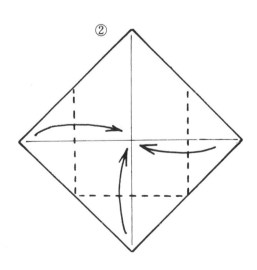

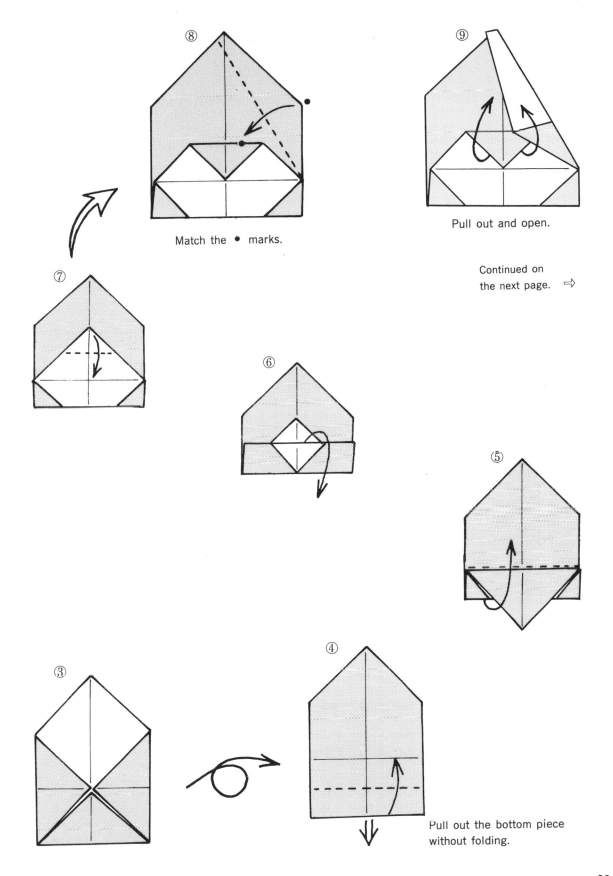

⑧ Match the ● marks.

⑨ Pull out and open.

Continued on
the next page. ⇨

⑦

⑥

⑤

③

④ Pull out the bottom piece
without folding.

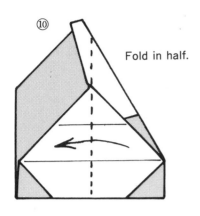

⑩ Fold in half.

Position reversed.

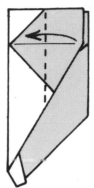
⑪ Fold the upper layer only.

⑫ Unfold.
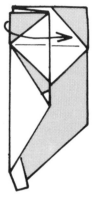

⑬
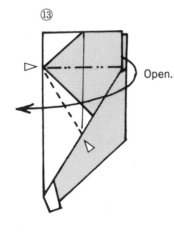
Open.

⑭
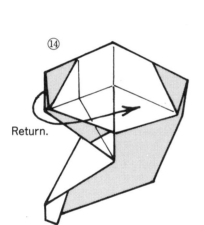
Return.

⑮
2

1

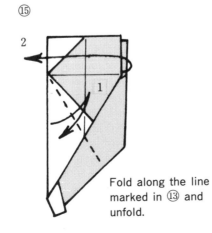
Fold along the line marked in ⑬ and unfold.

⑯ Lift.
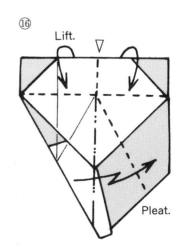
Pleat.

64

Inside pattern.

Outside pattern.

Pocket

Join the six units
as illustrated.

Tab

(Note) It is better to fold
and fix the ends after all
six units are joined.

Fix the end
by folding it
inside.

Finished unit.

Tab

Pocket

(×6)

Join as in the drawing.

65

Lid of a hexagon box : flower and star

Change the folding of the
units of the six-petal
pinwheel box so that the
inside pattern of the box
appears outside.

From ⑭ on page 64.

①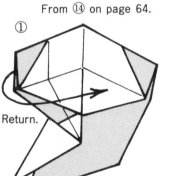

Return.

③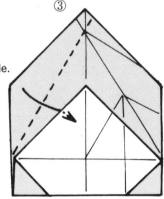

Tuck inside.

Turn
upside down.

②

2

1

Fold 1 and
then open.

④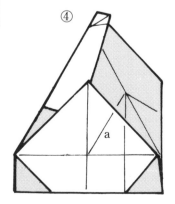

a

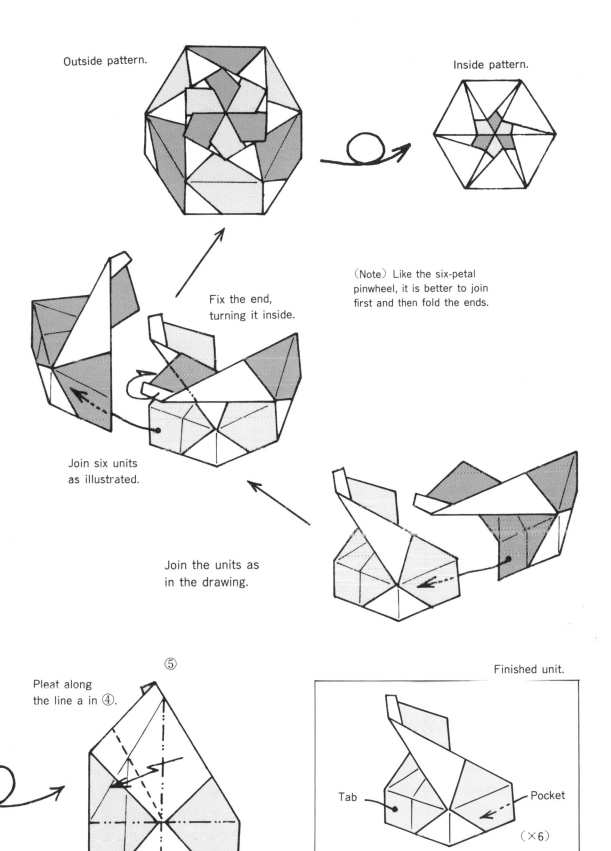

Outside pattern.

Inside pattern.

（Note）Like the six-petal pinwheel, it is better to join first and then fold the ends.

Fix the end, turning it inside.

Join six units as illustrated.

Join the units as in the drawing.

⑤

Pleat along the line a in ④.

Finished unit.

Tab

Pocket

（×6）

Base of a hexagon box

© 1988

Now we are going to make the bases for the two lids just made. In order to match the bases with the lids, the length of its six sides must be made shorter. The paper is folded up to ⑧ on the next page with this in mind. It is delicate work, so go slowly and patiently.

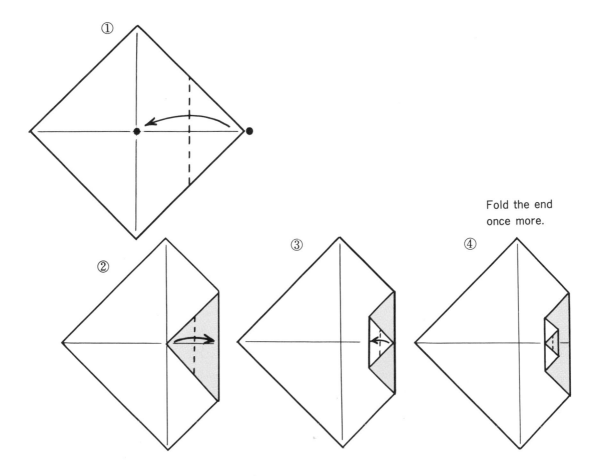

Fold the end once more.

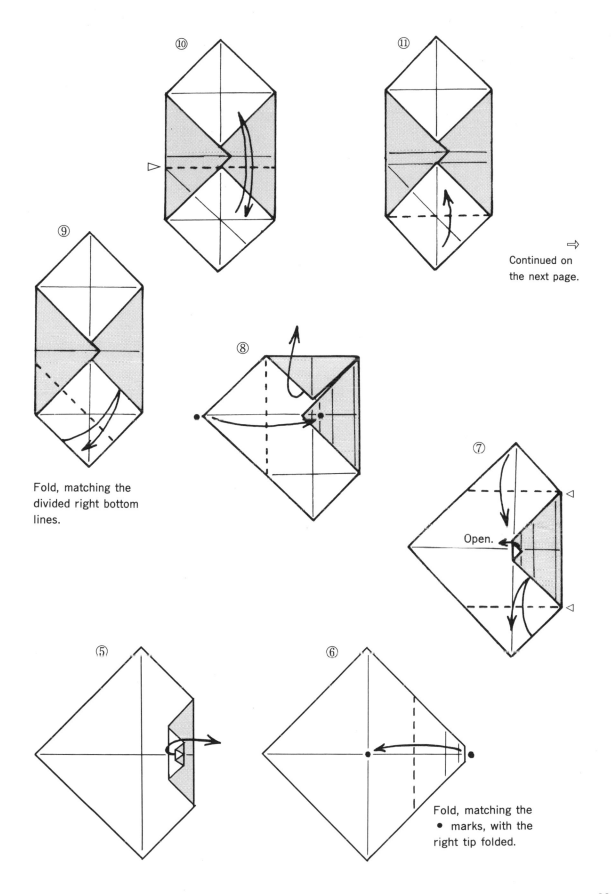

⑩

⑪

⇒
Continued on the next page.

⑨

Fold, matching the divided right bottom lines.

⑧

⑦

Open.

⑤

⑥

Fold, matching the
• marks, with the right tip folded.

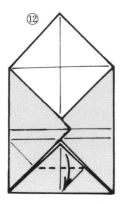

⑫

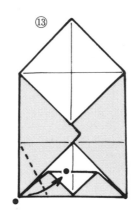

⑬

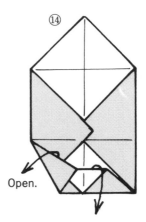

⑭

Open.

⑮

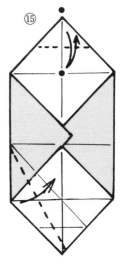

Fold along the
line marked in ⑬.

⑯

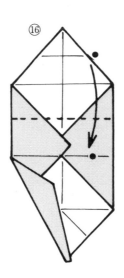

⑰

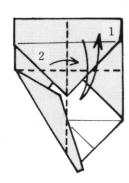

1

2

⑱

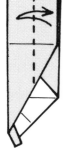

Fold the upper
layer only.

⑲

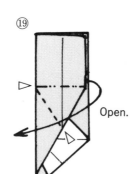

Open.

⑳

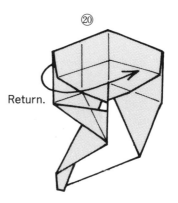

Return.

70

Inside pattern.

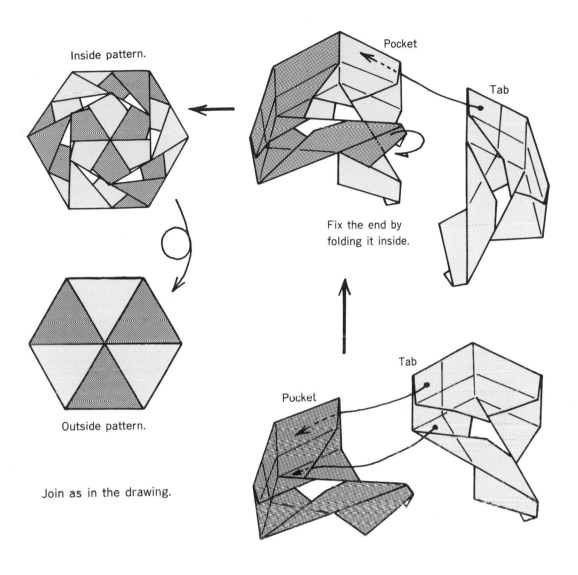

Pocket

Tab

Fix the end by
folding it inside.

Tab

Pocket

Outside pattern.

Join as in the drawing.

Fold along the
line marked in
⑲ and open.

⑳

2

1

Lift. ⑳

Pleat.

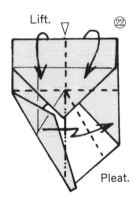

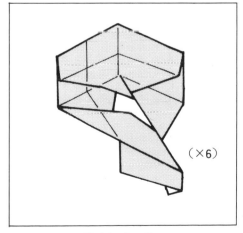

(×6)

Finished unit.

Here is how to fold the base of a hexagon box neatly with less time and trouble.

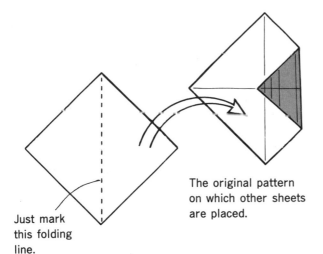

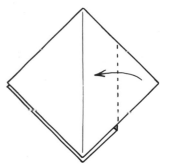

Just mark this folding line.

The original pattern on which other sheets are placed.

Fold according to the size of the pattern beneath.

When folding the base of a hexagon box, fold just one sheet up to ⑦ on page 69, use it as the original pattern, placing other sheets on it, and fold them according to the pattern beneath. This saves trouble. Moreover you do a neat job without folding unnecessary lines.